GETTING TO KNOW
THE U.S. PRESIDENTS

A N D R E W
JOHNSON

SEVENTEENTH PRESIDENT
1865 – 1869

WRITTEN AND ILLUSTRATED BY MIKE VENEZIA

CHILDREN'S PRESS®
A DIVISION OF SCHOLASTIC INC.
NEW YORK   TORONTO   LONDON   AUCKLAND   SYDNEY
MEXICO CITY   NEW DELHI   HONG KONG
DANBURY, CONNECTICUT

Reading Consultant: Nanci R. Vargus, Ed.D., Assistant Professor, School of Education, University of Indianapolis

Historical Consultant: Marc J. Selverstone, Ph.D., Assistant Professor, Miller Center of Public Affairs, University of Virginia

Photographs © 2005: Art Resource, NY/Alonzo Chappel/Smithsonian American Art Museum, Washington, D.C.: 4; Bridgeman Art Library International Ltd., London/New York: 25 (Alonzo Chappel/Chicago Historical Society, Chicago, USA), 29 top right (Courtesy of Historical Society of Pennsylvania Collection/Atwater Kent Museum of Philadelphia), 21 (New-York Historical Society, New York, USA), 23 (Private Collection); Capital Area Preservation, Inc./Mordecai Historic Park: 8; Corbis Images: 3 (Mathew B. Brady), 29 top left (David J. & Janice L. Frent Collection), 15; Getty Images: 32 (Library of Congress), 14 (MPI/Hulton Archive); Library of Congress: 6, 10; North Wind Picture Archives: 20; Peter Arnold Inc./Kim Heacox: 31; Stock Montage, Inc.: 29 bottom; Superstock, Inc./Collection of Archiv for Kunst & Geschlchte, Berlin, Germany: 5.

Colorist for illustrations: Dave Ludwig

Library of Congress Cataloging-in-Publication Data

Venezia, Mike.
   Andrew Johnson / written and illustrated by Mike Venezia.
      p. cm. — (Getting to know the U.S. presidents)
   ISBN 0-516-22622-3 (lib. bdg.)   0-516-25484-7 (pbk.)
1. Johnson, Andrew, 1808-1875—Juvenile literature. 2. Presidents—United States—Biography—Juvenile literature. I. Title.
   E667.V46 2005
   973.8'1'092–dc22

                              2004022560

$27.00

A photograph of
Andrew Johnson soon
after he became
president

Andrew Johnson was president of the United States from 1865 to 1869. He was born in Raleigh, North Carolina, in 1808. Andrew suddenly became president after Abraham Lincoln was assassinated. As president, he found himself facing an incredibly difficult job. He had to bring a badly damaged nation back together after its worst war.

Lee Surrendering to Grant at Appomattox, by Alonzo Chappel
(Smithsonian American Art Museum, Washington, D.C.)

The Civil War ended on April 9, 1865, when southern general Robert E. Lee surrendered to northern general Ulysses S. Grant. Everyone was relieved, but the country was left in a real mess. More than 600,000 lives had been lost during the Civil War. Cities and towns, crops, and livestock had been destroyed as well.

An illustration showing former slaves celebrating their freedom in 1865

No one was quite sure where or how four million former slaves would live, or what their rights would be. Some northerners wanted southern leaders to be punished, while others thought they should be forgiven. The process of fixing up the country was called Reconstruction.

Many southern cities, including Richmond, Virginia, were destroyed during the Civil War.

Abraham Lincoln had hoped the rebellious southern states would be brought back into the Union smoothly. Abe Lincoln was a strong leader and a genius at getting people to agree with each other. But Abe never got the chance to see if his plans would work. Unfortunately, it turned out that President Johnson wasn't as skilled a leader as Lincoln had been.

Andrew Johnson was stubborn and racially prejudiced. As president, he kept fighting with the U.S. Congress over how to handle Reconstruction, and very little was accomplished.

Andrew Johnson was born in this small house in Raleigh, North Carolina, in 1808.

When Andrew Johnson was growing up, his family was very poor. They rented a dirt-floor cabin that was on the property of a hotel. Andrew's father worked at all kinds of odd jobs at the hotel to scrape up enough money to feed his family. Sadly, he died when Andrew was only three years old. Now the Johnsons were *really* poor. Mrs. Johnson did her best to raise her two sons.

When Andrew was fourteen, he and his brother, Bill, were apprenticed to James Selby, the owner of a local tailor shop. Andrew learned to be an excellent tailor, even though he didn't like being stuck working in the shop all day.

An illustration of a tailor shop in the 1800s

Andrew did enjoy certain days, though, when readers would stop by. Readers were sometimes brought in to help pass the time in workshops. Andrew loved listening to the novels, plays, famous speeches, and newspaper stories that were read to the workers. Andrew had never spent even one day in school. Now, as a teenager, he had a great desire to learn to read on his own. Some of the readers were kind enough to help Andrew learn to read.

After two years of apprenticing in Mr. Selby's shop, Andrew and his brother decided to run away. The boys felt they were ready to make livings on their own. Andrew and Bill had broken the law, though. Mrs. Johnson had promised that her sons would apprentice until they were twenty-one years old. Mr. Selby was furious, and sent out "Wanted" notices offering ten dollars for the boys' return!

After a while, Andrew returned home and apologized to his boss. Mr. Selby didn't accept Andrew's apology, however, and hinted that he might try to get even with him. Andrew thought it might be a good idea to leave North Carolina.

Andrew convinced his mother, brother, and new stepfather to pack up and find a better life on the new frontier. So, in 1826, the Johnson family headed west. They stopped in Greeneville, Tennessee, where Andrew had some great luck. On his first day there, seventeen-year-old Andrew met Eliza McCardle, the girl who would become his wife. He found a job as a tailor, and even found a place for his family to live.

A portrait of Eliza McCardle Johnson

A year after he arrived in Greeneville, Andrew married Eliza McCardle. Eliza was the perfect wife for Andrew. She helped make up for all the schooling her husband had missed.

First, Eliza taught Andrew to write. Then she taught him arithmetic and more reading skills. Eliza was a good businesswoman. With her help, Andrew opened his own tailor shop. Soon he became very successful.

Andrew Johnson's tailor shop in Greeneville, Tennessee

Andrew's tailor shop became a gathering place for local townspeople. They enjoyed discussing politics and news of the day with Andrew. Andrew Johnson always felt that wealthy Tennessee landowners looked down on people with small farms and tradesmen like him. Andrew believed that more working-class people should be elected to government jobs and help run their towns and states. In 1828, Andrew decided to run for town alderman. At the age of nineteen, he won his first election.

This was the beginning of a very successful life in politics for Andrew. Two years later, Andrew was elected mayor of Greeneville. He went on to be elected to the Tennessee state legislature. Eventually, he was elected to the U.S. Congress, first as a state representative, then as a senator. Between his terms in Congress, Andrew Johnson even served as governor of Tennessee.

Andrew was never afraid to speak his mind about the rights of everyday working people. Many of Andrew's rich, well-educated opponents didn't like him at all. They made fun of Andrew's unschooled manners behind his back. Small-town and backwoods people always liked Andrew, though.

An illustration showing pro-slavery and anti-slavery citizens fighting with each other in the 1850s

When Andrew Johnson became a U.S. senator, the United States was about to split apart over what to do about slavery. Northerners wanted to end slavery, while southerners wanted to keep their slaves, and even spread slavery into new territories. Southern states were even willing to leave the Union to get their way!

Andrew was from Tennessee, a southern state. He had no desire to end slavery, but he definitely didn't want southern states to secede from, or leave, the Union. Just before the Civil War started, Senator Johnson frequently gave rousing speeches about the importance of keeping the United States together as one country.

A slave family picking cotton in Georgia in the early 1860s

Andrew Johnson always said he loved the U.S. Constitution and would give his life to keep the United States together as one country. People from the northern states thought Andrew was a great hero. People from the South thought he was a traitor. Andrew Johnson's life was now often at risk.

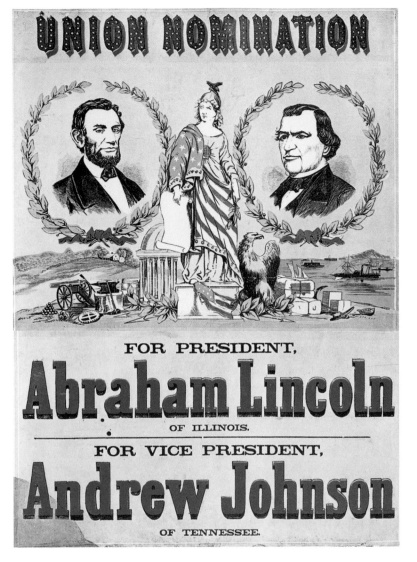

Once, a group of angry southerners boarded Andrew's train and threatened to hang him!

Somehow Andrew got out of the difficulty, but he and his family were always in danger.

Because of Andrew's loyalty to the Union, President Lincoln thought Andrew might make a great vice-presidential choice. In 1864, when Lincoln ran for a second four-year term, Andrew Johnson was his running mate.

Abe Lincoln and Andrew Johnson easily won the election of 1864. Almost immediately, a series of important events took place. A month after Abe and Andrew were sworn in as president and vice president, the Civil War ended. Then, only five days later, a horrible tragedy happened. An angry southern actor named John Wilkes Booth shot President Lincoln.

In Alonzo Chappel's painting *The Death of Lincoln*, Vice President Johnson (seated at left) waits somberly near the bedside of the dying president.

Abraham Lincoln died the next morning, on April 15, 1865. Later that day, Andrew Johnson became the seventeenth president of the United States. Andrew didn't have much time to think things over. Right away he had to figure out how to rebuild his country.

Unfortunately, President Johnson totally started off on the wrong foot. When he began his new job, the members of Congress were on recess. There was no one to check up on the president, so he did pretty much what he wanted. Some of the things Johnson did angered members of Congress.

First of all, President Johnson pardoned a

lot of southerners for the part they had taken in the war. He also ignored the rights of newly freed slaves. Many former slaves were being treated the same way they had been treated before the Civil War. When Congress came back into session a few months later, many Congressmen were very upset. From then on, Congress and the president fought constantly.

President Johnson didn't believe the U.S. government should be responsible for helping or protecting former slaves. He thought that job should be left up to each state. Most members of Congress disagreed. On one occasion, Congress wanted to pass a civil-rights law that would protect former slaves. President Johnson vetoed, or rejected, the law. Then members of Congress overruled the president's veto!

Finally, the leader of the House of Representatives, Thaddeus Stevens, said President Johnson should be impeached, or charged with serious misbehavior. Andrew Johnson ended up being the first president to be impeached.

Thaddeus Stevens (right) helped bring the impeachment proceedings against President Johnson. So many people wanted to watch Johnson's impeachment trial (bottom) that the Senate had to issue a limited number of daily admission tickets (middle).

To be taken up at MAIN ENTRANCE
U.S. SENATE
No. 16
U.S. SENATE

U.S. SENATE
Impeachment of the President
ADMIT THE BEARER
GALLERY.
APRIL 6TH 1868.
Geo. T. Brown
Sergeant at Arms.

When a president is impeached, the House of Representatives brings charges against him to the Senate. Members of the Senate then vote on whether to convict the president of any crimes. In this case, the Senate did not convict Johnson of any crimes. If it had, he would have been removed from office.

In spite of all the problems Andrew was having, one good thing was accomplished while he was president. In 1867, President Johnson's secretary of state, William H. Seward, bought 500,000 square miles (1,295,000 square kilometers) of land from the czar of Russia.

While Andrew Johnson was president, the United States bought the land that would become Alaska.

This region would someday become the state of Alaska. At first, Seward was criticized for wasting money on an area that seemed to have just ice, snow, and polar bears. Before long, though, people realized Seward had made a great deal.

A photograph of Andrew Johnson in 1868

When it came time to nominate a candidate for the next election, Andrew Johnson didn't stand a chance. Members of Congress felt he was totally unfit to be president. Voters pretty much agreed. Most people thought that the stubborn, self-centered president had kept the country from being rebuilt.

In 1869, Andrew Johnson left the White House and headed back to Tennessee. Years later, he was elected a U.S. senator from Tennessee. He died before his term ended, on July 31, 1875.